The Young Fabians

The Young Fabians are the under-31s section of the Fabian Society, Britain's senior centre-left think tank. Set up in 1960, we remain the only think tank run by and for young people. We are affiliated to the Labour Party and have formal representation on the Young Labour National Committee.

Our membership numbers over 1,000 and includes young professionals, students, parliamentary researchers, political activists and academics. All of the young MPs elected at the 1997 and 2001 elections were Young Fabians and, during those parliaments, there were more Fabian MPs than Tory MPs.

The Young Fabians develop policy ideas through seminars, conferences and pamphlets. We produce a quarterly magazine, Anticipations, and organise regular political and social events. We seek to encourage debate and political education amongst our members and within the wider Labour movement though campaigning and activism.

Find out more at **www.youngfabians.org.uk**

Fabian Society
11 Dartmouth Street
London SW1H 9BN
www.fabians.org.uk

First published 2007

ISBN 978-0-7163-2055-5

British Library Cataloguing in Publication data.
A catalogue record for this book is available from the British Library.

Stopping the Far Right

How progressive politics
can tackle political extremism

Edited by Fred Grindrod and Mark Rusling

with forewords from Graham Goddard
and Jon Cruddas MP

About the authors

Graham Goddard is Deputy General Secretary of Unite the Union.

Jon Cruddas is MP for Dagenham. Jon is Vice Chair of Labour Friends of Searchlight and between 1997 and 2001 he worked in Downing Street as a link between the trade unions and the Prime Minister.

Alessandra Buonfino is Head of Research at Demos. Prior to joining Demos, Alessandra was a Research Associate at the Young Foundation where she led on research focussing on far right extremism in Britain.

Meg Hillier was elected MP for Hackney South and Shoreditch in 2005 and is a junior minister at the Home Office. Between 2000 and 2004, Meg was a member of the London Assembly, representing Hackney, Islington and Waltham Forest. She writes in a personal capacity.

Nick Lowles and **Paul Meszaros** work for Searchlight, the organisation set up to counter racism and fascism in elections and beyond. More information can be found on their website www.stopthebnp.org.uk

Fred Grindrod is currently the Young Fabians Publications Officer. He is a member of the Labour Party's National Policy Forum and was Labour's candidate for Rochford and Southend East in the 2005 general election. Fred works as a policy manager at Crisis and was previously Senior Policy Advisor at the Commission for Racial Equality.

Mark Rusling is currently Vice Chair of the Young Fabians. He is the Campaigns and Education Officer for the United Nations Association of the UK, having previously worked as a Researcher for Linda Perham MP.

Contents

Acknowledgments

The editors wish to thank the following for their help and support in the realisation of this publication: Meg Hillier MP, Alessandra Buonfino, Nick Lowles and Paul Meszaros for their hard work in writing the chapters and Graham Goddard and Jon Cruddas MP for writing the forewords; Siobhan Endean, Vicky Foxcroft and Chris Weldon at Unite the Union for their sponsorship of the publication and assistance in developing its direction; Hannah Jameson and Tom Hampson at the Fabian Society for helping with the design, project management and layout; Nick Johnson, now at the Institute of Community Cohesion, and Patrick Diamond, now at the Commission for Equality and Human Rights, for their reviews of the initial proposal and for helping us to secure the authors; Jess Garland at Meg Hillier's office; Alex Baker for laying out the text at such short notice; Tom Flynn for suggesting the idea in the first place; Conor McGinn, Chair, and the rest of the Young Fabian Executive for their support throughout the year in getting this project going.

|Foreword from Graham Goddard

Unite the Union members have been working together with Searchlight to defeat the BNP where they have stood in elections. We decided that it is important to expose the insidious racism which runs through BNP policies, instead of offering solutions to the problems of job losses in manufacturing, education and housing - the BNP attempt to use these issues to cause division in our communities.

There is deep insecurity and poverty in many of our towns and villages, but the answer is to build a strong local economy where people have dignity and prospects of a secure job. The BNP preach a politics of hate towards Black and Asian communities and towards anyone who comes to live in our country. The resulting increase in racist attacks when the BNP get organised gives us reason to work together to ensure that they don't hold the platform of being elected to represent us.

It is young members of Unite that are the mainstay of our campaigns against the BNP. Treading the pavements on icy winter mornings to deliver leaflets and anti-racist information on your own can be a bit dull, but working together in groups makes all the difference. Unite have a strong young members' network which regularly works with Searchlight teams to campaign in local elections. I would encourage all young members to come along and get involved.

We also work to tackle racism when it appears in our workplaces - racist graffiti and comments have no role in the workplace and our members stand up to racism wherever it appears. Racism only thrives where there is a vacuum or where people are too scared to stand up to it. By working together - Unite the Union members, Labour Party members, and Searchlight - we can ensure that we beat the BNP wherever they stand.

Graham Goddard
Deputy General Secretary
Unite the Union

|Foreword from Jon Cruddas MP

The British National Party is beginning to establish itself as a rival to Labour in many of our traditional heartlands and there are strong signs that the BNP is becoming a home for many disgruntled former Labour voters.

Experience over the past few years tells us that local campaigning can defeat the BNP and help rebuild and reinvigorate local democratic politics; yet we must not just focus on defeating the BNP at election times, we must also confront the material conditions that lie behind its growing popularity. The BNP strategy is to be "more Labour than New Labour" so as to win support in traditional working class areas. Its manifestos often talk of "workers' ownership in a capitalist economy". It talks of standing for the values of "Old Labour" – by which it means the white working class. Every edition of its paper includes articles on business bullies, on Labour selling out British jobs and on how we are taking working class communities for granted. And it continually refers to the threats of globalisation, migrant workers and EU bureaucracy to reinforce the message that it is only the BNP that cares for British workers.

Young people in the Labour and trade union movement have a specific responsibility to confront the fascists. What is happening in the communities where the BNP is a threat is that a new politics is being forged;

anti-fascists and church groups, local union branches, voluntary and political groups are coming together in new creative ways to confront the far right.

Whilst all the political parties seek the vote of a specific minority of swing voters in a highly select part of the country, a new anti-fascist mobilisation is being co-ordinated by Searchlight to fight the fascists on a different political and geographical landscape. Searchlight is on the front line with new campaign techniques, innovative use of new technology, targeted mail, phone communication and voter identification, days of action and new forms of community engagement and activism. This anti-BNP work is having a lasting impact in our communities – many union activists have joined or rejoined the Party, new vibrant coalitions are being formed off the radar of the Westminster political classes; complex issues of demography, class, race, housing and public services are being worked through in a mature form often despite the contributions of national politicians whose interests lie elsewhere.

The BNP poses a serious threat to the Labour Party but it also gives us a unique opportunity to rebuild and reinvigorate our local organisations. Through fighting off the BNP we can do politics in a different way and reconnect with our traditional communities.

I am delighted that the Young Fabians have produced this pamphlet in conjunction with my union, Unite and I would urge members and activists across the movement to contact and contribute to the pioneering local work of Searchlight.

Jon Cruddas MP
Vice-Chair, Labour Friends of Searchlight
www.joncruddas.org.uk

1 | Introduction

Fred Grindrod is Publications Officer of the Young Fabians

The rise of far right extremists such as the British National Party has been one of the most worrying political trends of recent times. As I write this introduction in September 2007, the BNP are standing an unprecedented number of candidates in forthcoming local by-elections taking place in the North West, the North East, the West Midlands, the East Midlands and the East of England. With ever more candidates, increased media attention and a rising number of votes, the BNP seem to be developing into an insidious part of the political landscape.

The state of British politics, and social conditions in many areas of the country, have allowed the far right to grow. The BNP have successfully capitalised on the disengagement and disenfranchisement that many voters in deprived communities feel, as trust in politics and mainstream politicians has reached new lows. Many voters have become convinced that all politicians are elitist, deceitful and only "out for themselves", partly due to the negative images presented to them via the mass media. Our voting system focuses the main thrust of campaigning on the issues and concerns of those living in the "super-marginal" constituencies.

Such places are often a world away from the problems and aspirations felt in white working class areas, inhabited by those who rely on the state to provide decent services in order to gain a real quality of life. This campaigning frequently leaves white working class communities with a vacuum regarding who is really speaking for, and listening to, them. The BNP has been keen to fill this void.

Practically every day, the right wing press focuses its attention on issues that stoke the fears of communities - the so-called threat of the outsider; the problems of immigration; a Europe that is said to be determined to take every last vestige of identity away from us; and a Government that is supposedly desperate to steal our money, with stealth and death taxes round every corner. As the mainstream political parties, and particularly those of us on the left, fail to respond effectively with positive storylines regarding the truth, the BNP step into the breach and persuade people that they are the only ones still listening. Indeed, when the major parties capitulate to media pressure and try to appeal to the views of Fleet Street, the BNP step further into the limelight. People turn to the BNP first as a protest and then, subsequently, in the false belief that only the BNP can provide an answer to their very real problems.

The speed of change in our society contributes to these growing social problems. As some enjoy untold riches as a result of the strong economy, many feel left behind. As many benefit from the opportunities that 21st century Britain offers, many others remain trapped in isolated and often segregated communities. In an age of unprecedented globalisation, technological advancement and demographic change, many are left insecure and unsure of their place within modern Britain. For some, the BNP act as a false security with their easy lies, scaremongering and identification of scapegoats.

This publication, then, acts as a call to all those who espouse progressive politics to seek to reverse the rise of the far right. Our theme is that all on the left should be prepared to join the response to the BNP's challenge. Currently the threat of the BNP is being met by small teams of activists, often coalitions from within the communities afflicted, which struggle to cope with the increasingly efficient organising methods of the BNP. Although this work is being supported by trade unions and dedicated organisations such as Searchlight, we contend that more needs to be done. More help is needed from within the Labour Party and the wider movement.

We wish to engage the labour movement with the issues around the rise of political extremism in Britain today. Through a detailed look at the recent history of British far right politics, and a careful consideration of the current situation, we seek to engage all those on the left who are ideologically opposed to the BNP. If one is ideologically opposed to far right extremism, the appropriate response is to actively engage in the campaign against it. We also show that the Labour Party should be rising to this challenge - throughout its history, Labour has taken the lead in fighting those who would oppose equality, justice and freedom. Whenever fascism has raised its head in British political life, whether in the guise of Mosley or the National Front, it has been the Labour Party that has responded to this challenge and delivered real change for working people.

However, there is another reason for this pamphlet. Campaigning against the BNP can demonstrate the best of the labour movement to our society. Where active Labour parties and trade unionists have effectively campaigned and defeated fascists, they have often reintegrated themselves into their communities. Declining organisations, often losing or only just hanging on to local powerbases, have been able to transform themselves into effective campaigning machines and realistic voices for those they wish to represent. We explore how the labour movement, and in particular the Labour Party and trade unions, can campaign against the BNP and in so doing, engage more people and find new members. This publication will hopefully also act as a practical tool, drawing together young people, trade unions, and the labour movement as a whole to take on this fight.

We draw on a wealth of practical experience and knowledge in order to make our point. Alessandra Buonfino, Head of Research at Demos, has researched the subject of political extremism in depth and has published widely on it. Meg Hillier writes from her experience as MP for Hackney South and Shoreditch about how the speed of social change is impacting on working class communities in east London. Nick Lowles and Paul Meszaros from Searchlight examine the practical ways in which the labour movement can fight fascism and the far right. By demonstrating examples of successful activism from some of the effective campaigns that their organisation has been involved in, they provide a real toolkit for others to follow. We hope that you will do this.

2 | The stoppable rise of the BNP

Alessandra Buonfino is Head of Research at Demos and a fellow of the Young Foundation

The media is never short of stories on the British far right. Just this summer we were able to read about companies pulling out of Facebook because of links to BNP materials. We also heard about a fuel protest activist (who recently secured the BNP's best by-election result in its 25-year history after standing in Tony Blair's constituency) who left the party after a punch up. And then again we heard about the ex-BNP council candidate who had been jailed for stockpiling explosives in anticipation of a future civil war.

Yet, despite these kinds of stories, some media headlines have argued, and still sporadically argue, about the 'unstoppable rise' of the BNP, or emphatically suggest that 'one in four (people) may vote for the BNP'.[1] To most people in Britain these comments may sound like an exaggeration – and most often they are. But while the danger that the BNP represents politically is minor, the effects of the presence of the far right on communities in many of Britain's fast-changing villages, towns and cities are not to be underestimated. This chapter will provide a brief overview of the history and appeal of the main far right party in Britain - the British National Party - particularly, yet briefly, focusing on its strategies and appeal, its threats and dangers.

The British National Party: where it comes from and where is it going?

The British National Party was formed back in the 1980s as a clone of the National Front, and for many years it remained essentially a small, loutish group which – apart from a short victory in Millwall in 1993 – largely failed to make a real breakthrough in other areas. In 1999 the party had at most 1000 members. Yet when Nick Griffin became its leader, the BNP changed strategy. He embarked on a campaign to make the party more electable by shedding its extremism and racist image. Candidates swapped black shirts for suits and strengthened their campaign strategies. As Griffin argued in 2006: "To win electoral power, and to keep it, a political party needs to be rooted in a broad-based movement that is constantly developing and expanding the social and cultural bases of its support".

In order to widen its electoral base and appeal to more middle class voters, Griffin played down the racist overtones of his party (in favour of an outright argument for the need to dismantle multiculturalism) and introduced a full-on campaign for votes. A good website, door-to-door and face-to-face campaigning, a BNP magazine, a newspaper and even BNP TV helped him in his attempt at widening the support base. For many this realignment represented a move designed to position the BNP alongside more successful European far right groups, such as their French counterpart, the Front Nationale. Yet, compared with the Front Nationale and other far right parties in continental Europe (such as the Belgian Vlaams Belang or the Austrian FPO, for example), and despite Griffin's efforts, the British National Party has never reached a strong support base.

There is a variety of arguments which seek to explain the historic weakness of the British far right. Some political scientists stress socio-economic factors to argue that its low success is due to Britain being less affected than some European countries by sudden socio-economic changes, such as major depressions (for example, the Great Depression after the First World War). Others focus on political culture, stressing factors like the powerful sense of democratic values and the association of Britishness with anti-fascism. Others stress the importance of the First Past the Post (FPTP) electoral system which has an in-built disadvantage for smaller political parties. Others blame the poor performance of the BNP once its representatives are elected at council level. It is true that compared to other countries in Europe, Britain's far right parties remain electorally weak. However, its success in recent years, at local, mayoral and European elections, is significant for a number of reasons.

The number of people who voted for them and the number of fielded candidates have been steadily rising. At the last general election in 2005 the British National Party won 192,850 votes – a considerable number. In the 2006 local elections, the BNP fielded 356 candidates and increased their number of councillors from 20 to 49; in total, BNP candidates received around 235,000 votes. Geographically, these were concentrated in Birmingham satellite towns in the West Midlands, and some areas on the outskirts of London. By far the most significant, and much reported, breakthrough has been in Barking and Dagenham, where the BNP is now the second largest party, behind Labour. England First also made an unprecedented gain – winning two seats in Blackburn North, where the BNP came a close second in a further five wards. In the 2007 local elections the BNP fielded a record 750 candidates in an attempt to boost its 49 local council seats to around 100. But while its share of the vote was up in the North East and in Windsor and Maidenhead, there was little success elsewhere.

The presence of far right parties and activists can reinforce and provoke existing tensions, frictions and conflicts at the local level. It can reinforce hatred and make community engagement and dialogue very difficult to achieve. The presence of far right councillors can legitimise further far right activities, discrimination and racism and far right activity can lead to violence and can contribute to a rise in hate crime.

According to research conducted by Peter John et al (2006), the threat of the far right today consists in its appeal to disaffected citizens who are witnessing a changing Britain and do not feel listened to by mainstream parties. Polling evidence from the London Elections Study suggests that 23% of Londoners have either voted or would consider voting for the BNP in the future. This evidence is supported by the JRRT State of the Nation poll, which found that 24% of Londoners 'might vote' for the BNP in the future. These trends, coupled with the 2006 local election success that saw the BNP almost doubling its number of councillors, could further intensify local frictions.

How can we explain the success of the BNP?

Targeted campaigning succeeds when it focuses on more local rather than national issues (i.e. those issues motivated by people's concerns and beliefs about the areas they live in) and when it capitalises on conducive local conditions. These are predominantly areas that are segregated by race and faith (with a significant class divide); areas with a weak local leadership often witnessing the segregation of the voluntary sector or traditional networks of social support such as working men's clubs or church networks (particularly in poor white areas); and areas that have changed, and are changing, rapidly through immigration while doing badly in terms of crime, unemployment or service provision. The call to traditional white working class sentiments is strong in BNP campaigns and the emphasis on ethnicity, blood and nationalism is common in most of its literature. It tries to appeal to people's sense of belonging to long-gone white working class communities which are now fractured by change but which retain a collective nostalgia. The contraposition between the community that 'once was' and the one that is seen to make up Britain today is seen as a crisis.

In Barking and Dagenham, for example, where the BNP is the second biggest party, these overtones have had considerable success. The population has increased by 20,000 since 2001 (an estimate that does not include the number of people who are off the formal statistical baseline of the state), living in the lowest cost housing market in Greater London. In a place that experiences underinvestment, relative deprivation and fast change, understanding and coming to grips with diversity is hard and still represents a primary concern for the white working class of the east end. Immigration, as found by Peter John et al, appears to have become a symbol or focal point for various areas of concern such as stretched resources for the NHS and education; pensions and provision for the elderly; unemployment; and even charges for dental treatment and housing.

In a strategy that Searchlight calls the 'Big Lie', the BNP in 2006 falsely claimed that a secret 'Africans in Essex' scheme gave Africans £50,000 to buy property in the area. In Thurrock, the BNP falsely claimed that the local council had a secret deal with Hackney to transfer 3,000 asylum seekers to the area, playing on people's fears. By playing up to some people's negative perceptions of race relations or immigration or even the NHS, the BNP portrays itself as the most rational choice available to people. By offering to 'secure a future for white children', it aims to gather support for those who resent differential treatments. In 2006, in Sandwell, for example, the BNP falsely claimed a local library was going to become a mosque. As the BNP suggests on its website, "we don't hate anyone, especially the mixed race children who are the most tragic victims of enforced multi-racism, but that does not mean that we accept misgenation as moral or normal. We do not and never will".

Who are the people who are likely to support the far right?

The 2004 MORI Omnibus survey shows that, out of 96,400 interviewees, only 490 answered that if there were a general election tomorrow they would vote for the BNP or the National Front. These represented a mere 0.5% of the interviewees, although the proportion rose over the two year period of the survey. In general, studies show that far right supporters are most likely to live in urban areas and possibly in wards with a high percentage of ethnic segregation. Surveys show that they are relatively well informed and have strong political views (they are most likely to say that they voted at the last general election according to MORI), even if they don't engage much with their community. They are employed but have low levels of education and they have little contact with ethnic minorities in their daily lives.

The areas with strong support for the far right are identified by some studies as those constituencies that have at least one ward where 10% or more of the population is Asian and where 50% of the remaining wards are 90% or more white. This is backed up by the Home Office citizenship survey which shows that those living in multi-ethnic areas have more positive views towards ethnic minorities than those in mono-ethnic areas. Following the BNP's attempt to modernise under Nick Griffin, the party has also focussed its campaign on white rural villages by discussing local concerns around issues of lack of investment in the countryside and asylum seekers' accommodation centres.

During and after the 1990s, commentators increasingly stressed protest or anti-politics as the key factor explaining the rise of the extreme right. Many believe that parties like the BNP or the National Front (or even their continental European counterparts) lack any serious ideology and that their programme amounts to little more than a negative attack on the political establishment (even the immigration issue can be turned against elites by blaming past governments for laxity in this field). Most of the time extreme right supporters are merely seen as vehicles for expressing discontent with mainstream parties. Yet, this view is not entirely correct and is certainly not applicable everywhere. Alienation, deep feelings of voicelessness and instability and a difficulty to adapt to change, combined with the BNP's good campaigning strategies, can go a long way towards explaining the success of the far right in many British towns and cities. However, interpreting support for those parties as entirely 'protest-vote' is misplaced.

In many areas where its campaigns succeed, voting for the BNP is often seen as a perfectly rational choice and not entirely the result of 'the lack of an alternative' or a temporary protest. Dissatisfaction with main-stream politics certainly plays a part: a 2005 BBC ICM poll reported that 87% of respondents claimed that politicians did not keep the promises made before elections, while 9% said they never gave a 'straight answer'. As a result, voter turnout is affected – and tends to be lower in areas of above-average unemployment, below-average incomes and higher rates of economic and social inactivity. These tend to be tradi-tional Labour seats, and now many of them have turned into areas where the BNP campaigns.

In many of these areas, the main policy themes featured in BNP local manifestos are presented as appealing to the real concerns of residents. The BNP benefits from low voter turnout when it can capitalise on issues that are of sufficient salience to draw out voters. In Barking and Dagenham, for example, change has happened very quickly and there is a shortage of housing. In many areas around Britain there is a concern about paedophilia, immigration and crime. The BNP's success is in being able to capitalise on emotions and become the rational choice for people: in 2005, for example, in the BNP's strongest Burnley ward there was a 60% turnout. In that case, the BNP capitalised on fears of the potential risk of postal voting electoral fraud, which was explained by the BNP as an attempt by Muslim voters to cheat in elections.

While the BNP should not be taken too seriously in terms of their political impact, political parties, NGOs and public institutions alike should focus on what makes the BNP a potential threat. The local successes of the BNP are not just to be seen as temporary shifts or racist outbursts, but as symptoms that the bridge between people and politics is broken and that people find very few options to turn to when they try to make sense of a changing Britain. Re-gaining understanding, trust and those important personal relationships that should characterise politics is vital for fighting the stoppable rise of the British National Party.

3 | The British National Party: A view from the East End

Meg Hillier is MP for Hackney South and Shoreditch

It is easy to dismiss BNP supporters as simply racist - some no doubt are - but reasons for the party's support are more complex than racism alone. If we are serious about tackling the BNP, it is essential that we understand the reasons for its support.

From docks to docklands

Much BNP support has its roots in isolation, change in local communities and feelings of injustice. To understand these concerns in London and parts of the south east it is worth touching on the history of London's east end. The economic life of the east end over the last century has been a tale of two cities. Once a significant manufacturing base and an international trade hub, much of the work that was readily available for working class people was in the London docks. Manufacturing decline from the 1970s was a major contributor to the docks' closure in the 1980s. Docking, factory and warehouse jobs disappeared, leaving London's east end with some of the highest rates of unemployment in the country.

Jobs in the manual skilled trades had traditionally been gained through family connections. Sons followed fathers into trades, sometimes with cards being handed down in families. By 1980, large numbers of white men were out of work. Those out of work were not just white, but there are still jobs in London so family dominated that they are essentially white jobs. Take the Thames boatmen: until a very recent change in the law, there was a long apprenticeship which favoured family members learning on the job.

As the old east end industries died, a new economy was born within the City of London, which spread to the former docklands. The City thrived on the new knowledge economy with jobs in finance and communications. But those who had grown up in the east end were neither prepared for this new economy, nor educated to be part of it. Increasingly, people (including international migrants) commuted to the docklands from outside the area in order to fill the jobs, creating a divide between the working and the resident populations. Residents were not just white, of course, although many were poor and badly educated which meant that they were not able to benefit from these developments.

The Gherkin, a visual expression of London's global economic power, dominates the view from many Hackney and east end streets. It marks the divide between the old and new east end, representing a world a million miles from many of my constituents. Headteachers often tell me of school visits in which local children travel outside Hackney for the first time. In a recent survey of workers in Canary Wharf, only 33 came from Hackney. While Hackney's lack of a tube impacts on travel, the issue is more with the distances in expectation and educational attainment than it is with transport. Tower Hamlets council has developed some key links with Canary Wharf to try and boost the job prospects for their residents – with some success. The experience gap is crucial in tackling unemployment and in understanding what motivates some people to support the BNP.

Sometimes, having to adjust breeds resentment – and in London's cultural melting pot, with migrants from around the world, resentment can focus on race rather than the reality of the changing economy. Happily we are seeing a renaissance in Hackney schools. GCSE results have improved dramatically: in 2006 Hackney was one of the 10 most improved boroughs in the country. This year 54 per cent of Hackney pupils gained five or more A* to C GCSEs. It is vital that our children leave school with the right skills. Creating a highly skilled workforce is a passion for the Prime Minister and one we are right to pursue. Nevertheless, this drive for qualifications and skills leaves some groups feeling threatened.

Identity

There has been a well documented decline in the family ties that once bound together the white working class community of the east end. A seminal study by the Institute of Community Studies in the 1950s[1] showed the post-war east end community at the beginning of massive social change. At that time the east end was still a closely connected hub of extended family groups where married daughters lived near their mothers and sons followed fathers into their trade. There was also a very strong sense of solidarity and community; the 'blitz spirit' was still evident. Housing played a big role in strengthening and continuing the family groupings. Parents would recommend married children to private landlords when houses nearby became available. Children were far less likely to move away and families were critical in providing material security and support.

During the post-war period, as new council housing replaced the bombed slum terraces, many people were housed close to home. In Hoxton I know a number of old white east enders who have never lived more than a mile from where they were born. These people are often very isolated in today's Hoxton. They often feel hemmed in by new young families of different cultural backgrounds, with their own families living far away – because they now own their own home and have moved out or because they did not get a council tenancy. Others were rehoused outside London, away from family. This isolation is not caused by migration into Hoxton (most of which happened rather later), but this sense of isolation has been exploited by the far right.

Those who moved into the new estates after the war had shared hardship and experiences which created a community bond. Things are different now. In July I visited one of these post-war estates where older tenants were arguing that the council should introduce new tenants to their neighbours. An intergenerational dispute broke out. The older women wanted to know their neighbours; the younger women said that the world doesn't work like that anymore. But both realised that the lack of contact made it difficult to solve the small everyday problems of living close together. At that meeting, the mainly white attendees were speaking up for their neighbours who had poor English. Yet at meetings like this people often raise concerns about immigration – and they are not necessarily white. In Hackney the diversity of the population helps to combat the BNP and racism, at least it has in recent times. But it is not that long since the BNP had a hold in the former Metropolitan borough of Shoreditch (National Front chairman John Tyndall stood for election in 1979, gaining 7.6 per cent of the vote) – at a time when the post-war white tenants were seeing more international migrants live among them.

Many white Londoners followed the tube lines out east. By the 1980s, the loss of traditional jobs in manufacturing and the influx of professionals drawn in by the new economy saw the migration of many 'old' east enders out to Essex. Many of those left behind by the knowledge economy (including new migrants) remain trapped in welfare poverty.

The east London constituencies of Bethnal Green, Poplar and Canning Town and Hackney South are among the top 12 areas in the UK with highest unemployment. Hackney South has the second highest number of incapacity benefit claimants in London - 7,400.

At a recent constituency coffee morning I asked residents what messages they had for Gordon Brown, then a week into his premiership. One white British woman said: "Tell him to stop all these foreigners getting everything for free". She was speaking in a mixed group of residents. What was striking was that they all, migrants included, accepted that a fair and easy to understand immigration policy was a good thing. The overriding attitude was that the system needed to be fair – and the perception is often that some people are getting precedence over others in, for example, allocation of housing.

Currently there are over 80 different ways that someone who is not a European Union national can enter the UK legally. From 2008 the Government will roll out a new five tier system of migration. Those wishing to come to the UK will be able to apply in one of five categories: highly skilled workers; skilled workers with a job offer; limited numbers of low skilled workers needed to fill temporary labour shortages; students; and seasonal workers. We are also strengthening our border controls. UK visas now include fingerprints. We are piloting a new border control system which has led to 1050 arrests. We are also making our border controls more visible, with immigration officials in uniforms and a combined border control force which will incorporate revenue and customs and immigration officers. As we tighten controls we will be counting people out of Britain, making it much easier to catch those intent on staying here illegally and to measure the flow of workers and their contribution. The simple impact of having robust figures should help boost confidence among the general public and undermine those who spread scare stories about migration.

This visibility is important. People's perception (fuelled by some of the press) is that people are 'flooding' into Britain. The reality is that migrants contribute substantially to economic growth. Recent figures from the workers registration scheme (which covers eight of the ten countries which joined the EU in 2004) show that the numbers filling business and administration jobs have gone up to around 41 per cent of the total number of registered workers – because this is where the vacancies are.

One of the reasons for BNP support is that, for many, their perception is the reality, even if the facts say differently. This is a phenomenon that Frank Luntz highlights in his book 'Words that work'[2] - the argument of which is so well described in the book's subtitle, "It's not what you say it's what people hear". In challenging the BNP we have somehow assumed that just because we can rationally disprove their arguments, this is enough. Our challenge is that the BNP have reached out to people who (wrongly) have felt that we have abandoned them. Our task therefore is to combine the emotional argument (to show that we are on their side) along with a re-statement of the actual facts.

Migrants have over the centuries filled the jobs that others don't want. They still do to this day. Richard Florida in his work on the creative economy highlights clearly how modern migration is founded on the principles of creative clustering establishing a critical economic mass which is then sustained by migration, coming in to fill the key job shortages. London is one such city. It attracts a wide range of talent from around the world because of the coexistence of other creative people, academia and transport links. London needs that influx of talent to sustain its competitive edge, which supports the wider UK economy. So we need migration, but we should also understand that the consequences of that migration might have differential impacts on different communities in the UK.

Migration does affect our communities and public services. The Government has established the Migration Impacts Forum to examine the real impact. This is a very welcome step. When I was a member of the London Assembly we began an inquiry into the impact of migration on London's public services. But as we approached the 2004 London elections there was a cross-party nervousness about publication. We shared a concern about how any reasonable discussion would be presented publicly. The BNP gained 4.8 per cent of the London vote; 5 per cent would have gained it a seat on the London Assembly[3]. We need to have the courage to take on this debate. There are good socialist arguments for a fair immigration system. We must not cede the territory to the opposition and the far right. In the talk about demand on public services we should remember the contribution of migrant workers. One in four work permits issued in 2006 was issued to a worker in the health and social care sectors.

Unhappiness and insecurity

Over the years the east end has witnessed many cycles of integration through conflict, competition and eventual accommodation. Communities are changing faster than previously, creating challenges as public services work to keep up. According to the Commission for Racial Equality, almost half of migrants coming into the UK will leave again within five years.[4] This creates a challenge of churn, as well as raising questions about the buy-in of migrants to British society.

Where there are finite resources there will be competition and in recent years the focus of this dilemma has been housing. The issue of housing has sparked a debate about 'entitlement'. Barking MP Margaret Hodge has been criticised by many for suggesting that housing entitlement should be based on time spent in the local area. However, what she touched on reflects what many people feel. The woman at my local tenants' meeting was not alone in thinking that 'the foreigners' all get 'stuff for free'. While the reality is that housing is allocated according to need, we need a debate because perceptions are important and reflect what people believe are facts.

More are in need of housing than those defined as being 'in need' by the law. And 'need' is defined by the Government and housing authorities in such a way that housing has become unattainable to many people who, because of income, family or job, most would accept need afford-able housing (or who certainly cannot afford to enter the private markets). In 2000 I chaired a London Assembly inquiry into affordable housing. We made a point of interviewing frontline staff. Most aspired to become homeowners. We concluded that house prices led to a serious loss of middle management from London in a range of sectors. Many of my constituents want a home but cannot afford the private or supported ownership routes available. The mother of a local postman wrote to me, frustrated that her hard working son cannot get a home. He is single, so does not qualify for council housing. His income puts private renting beyond reach (rents are typically £250 to £400 a week for a one bed flat) and there is no prospect of a local mortgage. He is not 'in need' according to any social landlord in the land. Yet, patently, he is in need.

We inherited a depleted and neglected housing stock when Labour was elected in 1997. Then I could never tell anyone when their leaky windows would be replaced or if they would ever get a new kitchen. Now, thanks to Government investment, we have seen existing homes improved and know that the rest will follow. This emphasis on existing homes was necessary but it has meant that the march of household growth (and in London population growth) has increased demand for housing. Entitlement is an emotive issue and has the power to stir up deep feelings around the concepts of difference and Britishness. The BNP has sought to use these issues to stir up racial tensions. Housing is not an issue of race, rather of size and availability. Housing minister Yvette Cooper now attends Cabinet: a visible sign of the Government emphasis on housing. Her challenge is not just about building homes but ensuring there is a range of affordable options.

In the follow-up to the ICS research into post-war Britain, Geoff Dench et al[5] examined how many of those who had lived through the war in the east end saw the welfare state as their reward - a 'thank you' from government for their resilience. They believed that the benefits of the welfare state had been earned, and that they had a unique entitlement to it. Looking at it in these terms, it is easy to see how newcomers would not be seen as having the same claim on resources.

Interestingly, the BNP's support is in the London outer suburbs such as Barking – they don't have a foothold in multi-cultural, international inner London constituencies like Hackney. Much of the current debate and sources of tension about entitlement focus on the contribution made to Britain by migrants and their length of residency. This is not unique to the white community and is often a complaint levelled at new immigrants by more established immigrant communities.

It seems to derive from a very British concept – queuing. The charge levied at newcomers is that they have jumped the queue. There is an argument for more sophisticated lettings policies. Currently housing need is the mantra. On the face of it no-one would disagree. But if someone can care for their elderly mother if they live near, but not if they are five miles away, this could maintain a family bond, improve quality of life and save the public purse a great deal. And the needs queue can lead to some outcomes which none of us would say are desirable – where need overrides the benefits of a balanced community. On one large Hackney estate a local manager told me of the high number of ex-prisoners and people with severe support needs – all in general needs housing. Differentiated lettings are controversial and are not easy to introduce but we should not hide behind housing need as though that blanket of fairness somehow solves everything. It can breed the very resentment that leads people to seek other political outlets.

The Labour Party has always been on the side of the poor and now we struggle to connect with some. Do we really champion their priorities? I think we do – in areas like tax credits, good schools, anti-social behaviour, neighbourhood policing and many more. Yet, we need to be clearer about what we are doing and how, and to sell the message better. On a Hackney doorstep I have about a minute to explain a policy. People also need to believe that our actions will lead to results. Tackling the issue of available affordable housing is a crucial step.

Poverty and political support

Some working class people have turned away from Labour. And not just from Labour, but from politics more generally: the voting gap between manual and non-manual workers has more than doubled in the last two general elections. Some of these voters are not turning towards the Conservatives but to parties like the BNP which they believe represent their interests. Opposition to the system can easily be dismissed as racist but it isn't necessarily motivated in this way. At the heart is a community which feels that its needs are not being met. At the centre of the issue is the concept of fairness.

The Department for Communities and Local Government has been addressing these issues, establishing the independent Commission on Integration and Cohesion in August last year. It was asked to consider what local and practical action is needed to overcome barriers to integration and cohesion. Darra Singh, Chair of the Commission and chief executive of Ealing Council talked about building a sense of local identity as being key to the future. In London we see this clearly. In the past a Londoner was a white Cockney; now we are embracing a Londoner in an international context. The white 60 year-old born in Hoxton and the 20 year-old Nigerian-born woman are both Londoners. London is confident in these contrasts of experience and culture. The Prime Minister has emphasised the importance of a sense of Britishness and the Government is debating issues around earned citizenship. All these ideas are about community rather than race.

In his 1995 book 'Bowling Alone', American social scientist Robert Putnam introduced the concept of 'social capital' – the network of friends, neighbours, organisations and trust that builds up in communities and which we all rely on. He also talks of bonding and bridging capital. Within our communities we bond, but between communities we need to bridge. The latter can be more challenging. In his recently published study of social capital in the US he concludes that ethnic diversity reduces social capital – between and within ethnic groups. Putnam calls this withdrawal from connectedness in the community 'hunkering down'. He claims the effects of this are reduced political participation and confidence in government, reduced trust and sense of community and, ultimately, less happiness. But Putnam remains optimistic that such effects can be overcome. He stresses that they are short term consequences which change over time into new forms of social solidarity. He believes the solution to integration is not to "make them 'more like us' but to create a new 'we'". He sees the answer in civic education - defining what we have in common as well as our differences.

Defining Britishness is firmly on the Government and popular agendas but finding a concept that encapsulates our modern society is challenging. It is a mistake to make others conform to existing norms. Rather, we need a new forward looking concept of ourselves - not who we were but who we are going to be. This is easily said but much harder to achieve. We must not shy away from discussions of race and immigration and from recognising the concerns that people have. Only then can we tackle these concerns head on and demonstrate that we are the party for all groups and that we can meet the aspirations and tackle the fears of many of those who have found solace in the belief that the BNP is fighting their corner.

4 | Beating the BNP: A practical approach

Nick Lowles and **Paul Meszaros** work for Searchlight

The British National Party pose an increasingly serious threat, but they also provide opportunities for the labour movement. First, we must all accept that it is vital, politically and electorally, to confront the BNP. Secondly, we must use the BNP presence to our own advantage. Recent experience has shown that the BNP threat can galvanise party members and trade unionists, especially at a time when there is increasing disillusionment with the Labour government over domestic and international issues.

Defeating the fascist BNP is a clear and stark moral issue that can unite all sections of the labour movement, including the most disgruntled. Additionally, the threat posed by the BNP is quite different to that faced from the mainstream parties. This necessitates a different form of campaigning to that which has become increasingly the norm (which simply targets those who vote). This can only be good for our politics. Re-engaging with our voters and mobilising the labour movement are the themes of this chapter.

Anti-fascist activists and Labour coming together

Campaigning against the BNP has evolved over the last few years. At the beginning of this decade it was common for the anti-fascist campaign to be totally separate from the political parties and for its literature to be hard, provocative and sometimes hysterical. The political parties, and in particular the Labour Party, were hostile to our campaigning and took the general view that the BNP was best ignored. Over time these opinions have changed, and now there is a convergence of views – it is now seen that working together greatly improves our chances of defeating the fascists. Anti-fascists have learnt that, for the BNP to lose, a political party has to win. Meanwhile, the Labour Party has increasingly accepted that fighting the BNP can energise activists in a way that the Government's public sector reforms cannot, and that anti-fascists can sometimes reach sections in the community that the party cannot engage with at present.

More fundamentally, there is also the growing acceptance that defeating the BNP requires the normal party handbook to be discarded. Whilst out campaigning in a council by-election in Yorkshire in 2002, a Labour Party regional organiser dissuaded party members from leafleting three tower blocks in the centre of the ward. "It's a waste of our time leafleting there," he told us. "In the first only 11 people voted last time, in the second seven and in the third just three." With forty flats in each block he simply thought that he was saving precious time by ignoring those who do not normally vote. It is a tactic that has become increasingly common with all three main political parties. However, it is a strategy that simply does not work, as the BNP galvanises those who do not normally vote, especially those who believe that they are being ignored by the main political parties, particularly Labour. By focusing just on those people who normally vote, Labour is merely re-enforcing the perception that they do not care and is ignoring having to address the reasons why people are not voting. Fortunately, an increasing number of people understand that the targeting strategy cannot work in relation to the BNP. The alternative, though more labour intensive, not only removes one of the reasons why people vote for the BNP but, more importantly, helps Labour re-engage with the very people who have left them over the last few years.

The first example of where this new form of politics worked was in Dagenham, east London. In the run up to the 2005 general election, the BNP viewed this constituency as their principal London target. The fascists had just polled over 50% of the vote, a record for the BNP, in a council by-election in the area, and its 14.8% share across the borough in the European elections the previous year was its highest in the country. Rather than ignoring this threat, as was then the norm within the party, Dagenham CLP and its local MP Jon Cruddas took the BNP on. A packed all-members meeting early in the New Year galvanised local activists and union members. Movingly, it was to be the great trade union leader, Ron Todd's last public appearance before his tragic death of cancer. He stood up from the floor, recounted his own battles against Mosley's Union Movement in the 1950s, and explained how we must confront the BNP today.

In mid-March, two months before the general election, a Searchlight Day of Action was held in the borough. A staggering 148 people attended and 42,000 newspapers were delivered. Most of the people who came along were Dagenham Labour Party members and trade unionists, particularly from the local GMB. Food was provided and many activists joined, or rejoined, the Labour Party as a result. Unfortunately there was not the same response in neighbouring Barking CLP, for which they were to pay the price. While Dagenham Labour Party used the threat of the BNP to energise its activists and rebuild its organisation, the opposite was true of Barking CLP. The result was that the BNP polled 16.7% in Barking, its highest vote in the country, whilst gaining only 9.8% in Dagenham, despite the latter constituency being, on paper, more promising for them. The BNP recognised the resistance being put up in Dagenham and subsequently switched their focus to Barking, where they went on to gain 11 councillors the following year.

In Keighley, West Yorkshire, where Nick Griffin was the BNP candidate in 2005, over 25 different targeted leaflets were delivered before a massive day of action. The whole constituency received a hand-delivered copy of a Searchlight special tabloid. Local anti-fascists worked hand in glove with Labour and were able to mobilise scores of trade unionists to do likewise. Griffin came last with 9% of the vote, and Labour held this marginal seat with an increased majority.

Working with Searchlight

By 2007 Searchlight was working closely with the Labour Party across the country. The BNP was becoming an increasing threat and there was a shared realisation that we needed to work together more closely if they were to be defeated. We were also joined by an increasing number of trade unions who, having taken the BNP on for several years, had not really been integrated into the general anti-BNP campaign. Now we were all working together and the results of the 2007 council elections were evidence of our success. The BNP went into the polls with a target of 70 wards which could have been won on a swing of 5% or less. Even on the eve of the election, BNP leader Nick Griffin was confidently predicting on the party website at least 30 gains, though he suggested that they could win as many as 60. They ended up with a net gain of zero, a truly fantastic result for us. More importantly, the BNP slipped back badly in many of its core areas.

One of these areas was Sandwell, in the West Midlands. In the 2006 local elections, the BNP averaged 33% in the nine wards it contested, making it their strongest area after Barking and Dagenham. In several of the wards the BNP polled in excess of 40%. Fortunately, the local Labour

Party took the BNP seriously and, under the direction of the council leader, they established a working group and ordered their candidates and councillors to increase their activity. A worker was hired by the Labour Group to help co-ordinate campaigning in West Bromwich West and Searchlight was brought in and a strategy devised.

The election campaign kicked off with a Searchlight Day of Action, where over 220 people helped deliver 45,000 tabloid newspapers in one day. The paper was customised for Sandwell, with a story of a local BNP councillor who had his pub closed after a series of violent incidents during which he refused to collaborate with police. The Daily Mirror's 'Hope Not Hate' bus took activists to the local market and a local steel band played to shoppers where we were able to engage with local people. The day brought party members, trade unionists and anti-fascists together and created a momentum for the rest of the campaign. Many of those who came out for the day of action for the first time helped during the campaign. This was especially true of the trade unionists, who were much more integrated into our campaign than in previous years.

Unite led the campaign locally. They wrote to all their members advertising the Day of Action, distributed anti-BNP material internally and produced a DVD pushing for a Labour vote which was sent to all 9,000 members in the borough. On election day several of their full-time officers helped increase the Labour vote and their telephones were put to use in identifying anti-BNP voters. It was a campaign unrivalled by any union anywhere in the country. The success of Sandwell was due to the fact that it was an organised and integrated campaign. By campaigning locally, Searchlight identified and targeted BME voters in key wards and the unions mobilised their members. We telephoned voters, sent letters and contacted them again on polling day. The results were testament to the extra work put in during this year. The BNP failed to win a single ward and their vote was slashed. In one ward, Great Bridge, the BNP vote was cut from 45% to 30%, whilst in two others Labour gained an extra 400 votes.

It is important to stress the role of young people in the anti-BNP campaign. Time and again it is the younger generation who have provided the foot soldiers for our campaigns. London Young Labour has found that mobilising against the BNP has helped build their activist base significantly. On one day of action in Dagenham earlier this year they had 60 people out canvassing and leafleting. During the recent local elections they adopted Thurrock as their base of operations (there were no elections in London) and day after day helped build the Labour vote. On election day itself, over 40 Young Labour members got people out to vote Labour. Helping Labour in wards threatened by the BNP has proved a great way to encourage activism and build Young Labour. Labour Friends of Searchlight is keen to extend this to other areas of the country and to particularly target Labour Clubs at universities and colleges, where we should be able to mobilise activists around combating the BNP.

The importance of unions

The importance of integrating the unions into the wider anti-BNP campaign is best exemplified in Yorkshire which, until the 2007 elections, had the biggest concentration of BNP targets (and candidates) in the country. However, while they remain a very serious threat, they again failed to make any significant breakthrough. This is largely due to the great work of the Hope Not Hate Campaign in Yorkshire which helped co-ordinate the campaign locally. Hope Not Hate, Yorkshire works closely with the Yorkshire TUC, through which all the major unions endorse and back the campaign. Two brief examples from Halifax and Bradford show what can be achieved when we campaign together.

The Pennine town of Halifax was one of the first places in the county to see BNP breakthroughs and, although a lot of anti-BNP activity took place, it did not appear to be effective. In Illingworth and Mixenden we had a situation where the death of a local Labour Councillor, Tom McElroy, and the resultant by-election left a threat of the BNP holding all three seats in the ward. From the beginning, the local party (including the MP, activists and the district party) decided to work closely with Hope Not Hate, Yorkshire. We were determined from the outset to run a co-ordinated strategy that would bring party activists, trade unionists and anti-fascists into a coherent focussed campaign. Anyone who was serious about stopping the BNP was by now mobilised behind the Labour Party campaign.

The campaign was carefully planned with Hope Not Hate, Yorkshire to coordinate Labour activity and third party interventions. A Labour leaflet would be followed by an anti-fascist leaflet, layering the message that the BNP was bad news and could be defeated by Labour. This took place alongside constant canvassing work. The trade unions provided a core of activists to help with deliveries and door knocking. They also funded several targeted mailings to voters. Tom McElroy's own background as an active trade unionist sat well with a labour movement-led campaign, and it was easy to use his legacy in anti-fascist leaflets.

This co-ordinated approach quickly proved effective. The BNP ran a sophisticated campaign; they put out several leaflets, canvassed and sent direct mail to their supporters. We established from the outset that this was a straight fight between the BNP and Labour and that the way to beat the BNP was to vote Labour. Election day itself was hugely busy and effective. Activists from Labour, the unions and the anti-fascist movement across West Yorkshire came to help. Door knocking went on from dawn to dusk, with the candidate being accompanied by the local MP. Voters received a letter from Ross Kemp, and a recorded phone call from Liz Dawn.

The by-election in February 2007 was, as predicted, a close run thing. The BNP knew that they had 1,000 votes and that they were sufficiently organised to mobilise those voters, but Labour nevertheless beat them by 70. The momentum and self confidence gained from this victory carried through into the May elections where Labour won more decisively, by 400 votes. Over the course of a year, the share of the Labour vote increased from 28.6% to 42.5%. Not only were all sections of the Labour movement mobilised behind the campaign of Hope Not Hate, but voters were given a positive and visible alternative to the BNP. Prospects for the BNP in this area now appear bleak.

Another area that has seen successful campaigning is Bradford South. Although initially reluctant to challenge the BNP head on, the local party has risen to the challenge of beating one of the more combative BNP branches. Over the last two years, the BNP vote has been driven down, as Labour victories have increased. By working closely together we have ensured that the positive Labour message, together with the message of Hope Not Hate, is directed at those key groups of voters necessary for us to win. The trade unions are also given a clear steer as to where to concentrate their efforts, and have responded by setting up leafleting and canvassing teams, staffing telephone banks and paying for targeted mailings.

Regular activity in these areas has been augmented by days of action around, for example, Yorkshire Day. Last Yorkshire Day saw a large mobilisation of party activists, union members and students from the recently reformed Labour Club keen to get involved in the fight. Whilst one leaflet can only achieve so much, we have seen some culture shifts through this kind of work. In Tong, a ward in Bradford South, anti-fascist activists had been chased off the streets, racist attacks were common on the estates and the BNP vote peaked at 32% in 2006. Labour councillors in this ward have taken a strong anti-BNP stance in their literature, as well as working hard in the ward throughout the year, tackling tricky issues head on. In 2007 the BNP vote fell by over 10% and Labour defeated them with a resounding majority of 800 votes.

Less than a fortnight after Yorkshire Day, the local paper reported another racist attack on an Indian family returning to live in Tong. The Bradford woman's house and car were daubed with racist and neo-Nazi slogans and swastikas within a week of their arrival. Yet the local, predominantly white, community was quick to defend the family with a petition condemning the vandals. One local resident said, "This kind of hatred doesn't stop here. It affects everyone. It is a form of pollution. If good people do nothing, evil prevails. Everyone here is unanimous in condemning this and we feel we should stand up and be counted."

The BNP is in retreat in those areas where co-ordinated campaigning has taken place. The legacy is also one of stronger and more self assured local parties, confident in their abilities to face further challenges. Those communities once threatened by the BNP are returning to Labour now that we are once again visible on their estates. The party has recruited from amongst anti-fascists - those who have seen that a united labour movement response to the BNP was the thin red line that held the Nazis at bay.

5 | Conclusion: Labour at the forefront of anti-racism

Mark Rusling is Vice Chair of the Young Fabians

T he Labour Party has a proud history of standing against those who wish to discriminate and divide society along the lines of race. Although Labour governments have generally sought to restrict immigration, they have also attempted to improve conditions for minority communities living in the UK. All members of the labour movement should build on this history of tolerance and solidarity to engage in the struggle against the BNP, not just ideologically, but also through practical campaigning. This is, as Searchlight explains, "a clear and stark moral issue" – although the BNP may have had a minor political impact, the social impact of local BNP activism can be devastating.

There has never been a racist faction in the Labour Party and, throughout the Party's history, the vast majority of Labour members have always viewed racism and racist politics with disgust. Examples from Labour literature and legislation from the 1950s to the 1970s show this very clearly. As early as 1958, Party literature declared that the "Labour Party utterly abhors every manifestation of racial prejudice". Shameful episodes such as the racist Conservative 1964 election slogan, 'If you want a nigger for a neighbour, vote Labour' are rightly alien to the Labour tradition, which sees the nation in social, rather than racial, terms.

However, Labour's history should not lead us to be complacent about the need openly to resist and to combat the racist and discriminatory message of the BNP. We must never fall into the trap, identified by Shirley Williams as being prevalent within Labour's intellectual left-wing, of romantically assuming that British working people are incapable of intolerance or racism. We must expose the BNP's lies when they make claims such as 'Africans in Essex'. However, we must also seek to address the causes of the social upheaval and political disengagement that the BNP exploit in areas such as the East End, Barking, Dagenham, West Yorkshire and the West Midlands.

In government Labour has consistently sought to improve the life chances of all minority communities. This has been achieved through targeted anti-discrimination legislation and through improving conditions for all those living in poverty in Britain. Labour's NEC first declared its support for anti-discrimination legislation in 1962, and the Wilson government was the first to outlaw incitement to racial hatred in public places through the Race Relations Act 1965, which also established the Race Relations Board.

In 1968, the prohibition on discrimination was extended to private life through the provision of goods, services, facilities, employment, housing and advertising. The newly-established Race Relations Commission was also given the power to initiate its own inquiries, allowing it proactively to take the fight to those who would discriminate on the basis of race. Labour has always attempted to use legislation to undermine racist views and behaviour, and in 1976 created the Commission for Racial Equality, with a wide-ranging brief to eliminate discrimination, promote racial equality, encourage racial harmony and provide education on race issues.

Labour can be justly proud of its history of progressive legislation on race relations. However, this legislation cannot in itself combat the attitudes which lead to support for racist parties such as the BNP. Persistent activism, inspired by the values shown in Labour's anti-discrimination legislation, is needed from Party and trade union members to combat the BNP's attempts to divide British society on the basis of race. As Searchlight has argued, our campaigning needs to focus not only on target voters in swing seats, but on all those who are currently disengaged and disenfranchised. By linking Party and trade union members with anti-fascist groups such as Searchlight, Labour can reinvigorate its local parties by reintegrating them into their communities.

Thirty years ago, a discussion paper sent to every Constituency Labour Party argued that the "racist parties in Britain project themselves as down-to-earth working class organisations". What was true of the National Front in the 1970s is equally true of the BNP now. Labour and the trade unions must actively resist the BNP's attempts to turn the white working class against the equally-poor non-white working class. As the Labour Young Socialists wrote in 1973: "Rather than causing the problems of the working class, as a minority within that class [black] workers suffer the most".

In addition to promoting anti-discrimination legislation, Labour governments have tried to alleviate poverty among all communities in the UK. Labour's policy, as stated in 1977, remains true today:

"Any child, black or white, attending schools which are handicapped by inadequate buildings, overcrowding, lack of resources and high staff turnover in an environment of poor housing, poverty and social neglect will start with the odds against them...Racist parties deliberately exploit every difficulty we face – unemployment, overburdened social services, poor housing and high crime rates – and claim these are caused by black people".

Labour's history of standing against racism and discrimination should spur today's activists to oppose the BNP – the current manifestation of these attitudes – both ideologically and practically. Despite swapping skinheads for suits, the BNP remains an intensely racist and anti-democratic party. Labour should not treat the BNP in the same way as we would treat our mainstream political opponents – their ideology and political methods do not merit that respect. We should always seek to undermine their credibility as a party that can improve the lives of people in working class communities. We must address the concerns, over issues such as housing and immigration, which make voting BNP appear a rational choice to many people. In doing this, we will convince working class people that it is Labour, and not the BNP, that is fighting their corner.

Although we must be aware of the superficial attraction that the BNP's simple message may have for some traditional Labour supporters, we should not pander to that message by being coy about the values that have informed Labour legislation and literature. We should be proud of these values, and should not be afraid of stating them explicitly. As the Party stated in 1968: "we...must show our abhorrence of [racism] and try to remove it from our society. Equal opportunity means equal opportunity for all people, whatever their differences in skin, colouring, ethnic background or religion".

While Labour must never neglect the working class people of all races and religions who have been the Party's natural supporters, we should never fall into the trap of seeing multi-racial Britain as a threat, rather than as an opportunity. The values of tolerance, non-discrimination, cultural diversity and a commitment to equal opportunity, regardless of race, are Labour values. They are not practised by the BNP. Supporting the ideals that have sustained Labour throughout its existence means rejecting the BNP, both ideologically and through practical campaigning. Every Labour and trade union member should join this fight.

References

Chapter 1

1   The Sun, 2006.

Chapter 2

1   Michael Young and Peter Willmott, *Family and Kinship in East London*, 1957.
2   Frank I. Luntz, *Words That Work: It's Not What You Say, It's What People Hear*, 2007.
3   In the event UKIP was the surprise winner of two seats, benefiting from the fact that the London and European elections were being held on the same day. This will not be the case in 2008.
4   CRE internal analysis of 2004 ONS data.
5   Geoff Dench, Kate Gavron, and Michael Young, *The New East End – Kinship, Race and Conflict*, 2006.

INSIDE
Interview with Ed Balls MP
Coverage of the French election
Examining Labour's policies on crime

YOUNG FABIANS

ANTICIPATIONS

Has Labour got the bottle?

**We look at the progressive policies you think Labour
should have introduced, and ask why they haven't**

Spring 2007
Volume 10, Issue 4

INSIDE
On why women make better leaders
The quest for a green leader
How Labour's election process needs to change

YOUNG **FABIANS**

ANTICIPATIONS

Follow
my leader
An Anticipations leadership special

Autumn 2007
Volume 11, Issue 1

Fabian Review

FABIAN CONFERENCE SPECIAL

www.fabians.org.uk

Winter 2006/07

BUT WHAT WOULD HAVE TO CHANGE?

The next decade
Five challenging essays on foreign policy, education, life chances, democracy and the environment.

The Fabian Interview
Balancing Westminster and west Yorkshire. A day with Yvette Cooper in Labour's heartland.

The quarterly magazine of the Fabian Society   Volume 118 no 4   £4.95

Fabian Review

www.fabians.org.uk   Spring 2007

THE ENVIRONMENT SPECIAL

GREENING POLITICS

BUT WHICH VISION WILL DO IT?

PETER HAIN
ELLIOT MORLEY
MICHAEL MEACHER
EMILY THORNBERRY
CHRIS HUHNE
TIM SMIT
JEFF ZITRON

What does red-green really mean?
David Miliband sets out his 'next
decade' vision of the environment

Progressive or prophet of doom?
Matthew Taylor asks Mayer Hillman
whether we can live up to him

PLUS: Women's votes will decide the next general election, says Seema Malhotra

The quarterly magazine of the Fabian Society   Volume 119 no 1   £4.95

The Fabian Review, Spring 2007

JOIN THE YOUNG FABIANS TODAY

Join us and receive two copies of *Anticipations*, plus invitations to all Young Fabian events, and copies of all Fabian Society membership publications.

I'd like to become a Young Fabian for just £5

I understand that should at any time during my six-month introductory membership period I wish to cancel, I will receive a refund and keep all publications received without obligation. After six months I understand my membership will revert to the annual rate as published in *Fabian Review*, currently £31 (ordinary) or £14 (unwaged).

Name   Date of birth

Address

                                              Postcode

Email

Telephone

Instruction to Bank   Originator's ID: 971666

Bank/building society name

Address

                        Postcode

Acct holder(s)

Acct no.   Sort code

I instruct you to pay direct debits from my account at the request of the Fabian Society. The instruction is subject to the safeguards of the Direct Debit Guarantee.

Signature   Date

Return to:
Fabian Society Membership
FREEPOST SW 1570
11 Dartmouth Street
London
SW1H 9BN